I0782676

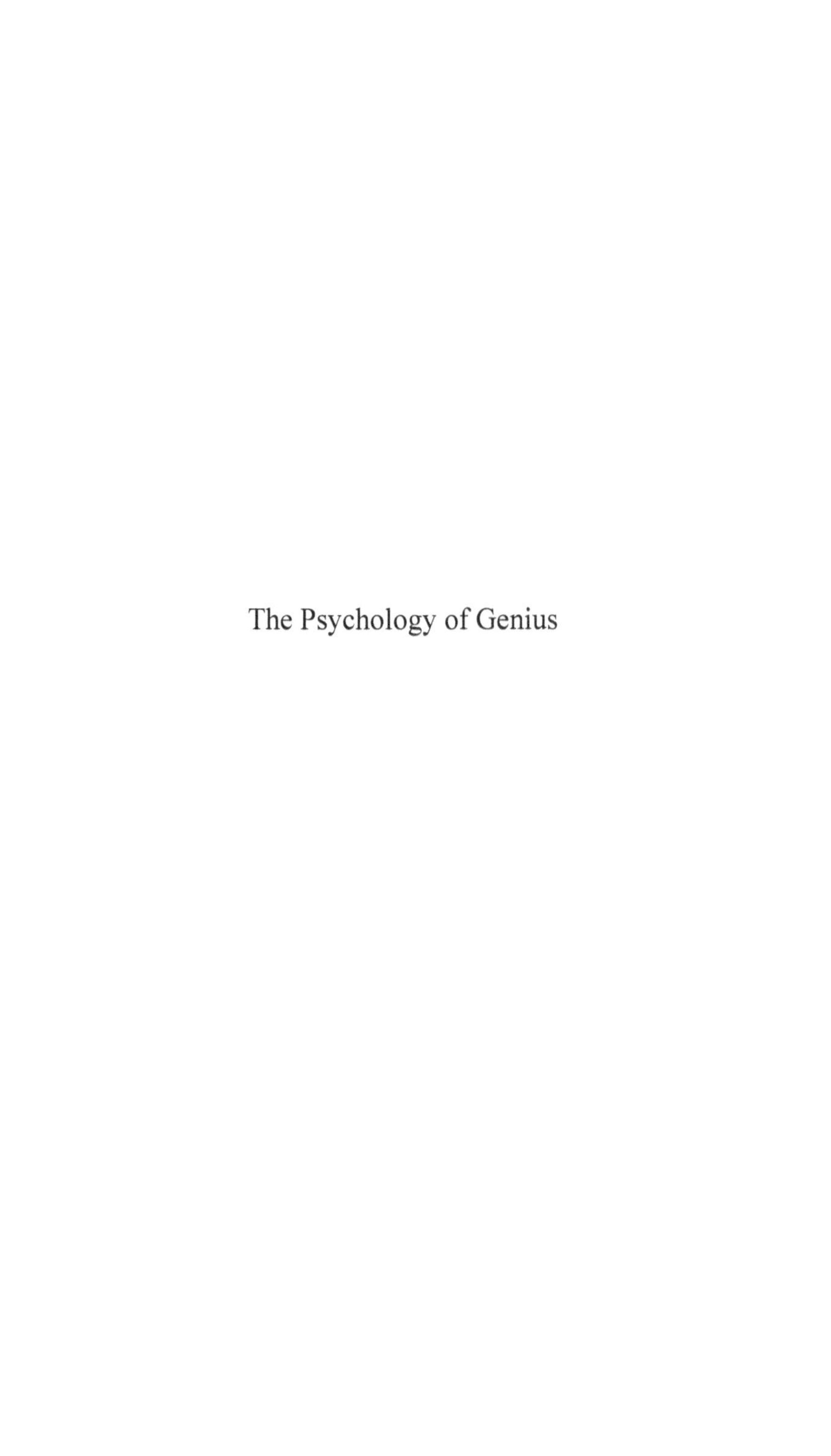

The Psychology of Genius

The Psychology of Genius
Genius and Insanity

Sully James

William Hirsch

The Psychology of Genius[1]

Our knowledge of the physiology of the human body has been so much enriched by pathological facts that we may truly say that some branches of it would, as far as we can see, have remained forever closed books if the effects of disease had not been observed. So it is with psychology in its turn. Since mental disease has been systematically studied, the science of the mind has undergone a veritable revolution. Having laid down its conceptions and having learned that psychical processes, like all

---

[1] By William Hirsch.

other phenomena of Nature, are subject to definite law, psychology has made an effort to determine the law of the mental processes of genius and to frame a definition of genius that should take into account facts which are now scientifically established. Many attempts have been made to determine what genius is, from which various conclusions have resulted, but those inquirers who have sought to penetrate to its psychological laws and to explain its phenomena upon recognized psychological principles have been obliged at last to acknowledge that they had to do with the most diverse psychological conditions which have been promiscuously labeled as genius.

The question whether the popular word genius can be used as a scientific term can be decided only by a psychological analysis of those poets, painters, virtuosos, scholars, statesmen, and generals who have been generally recognized as geniuses. Famous poets, observant of their own inward conditions, have often said that their works were composed as in a dream, unknown to themselves; that instead of being deliberately constructed, their ideas have, as it were, flown to them.

Involuntary thought is frequently described by the poets as unconscious. That can not be accurate, for "unconscious thought" is a contradictory phrase. Not even a dream can be said to be unconscious, whether it be purely ideal like most dreams, or produce action as in sleepwalking. In such a state self-consciousness alone is suspended, not consciousness itself. Fancy stands halfway between dreaming and active intellectual function. The latter depends directly on the will, while in the former the will is in total abeyance. All men are subject to fall under the influence of fancy. In ordinary men it makes day-dreams, which everybody recognizes to be opposed to purposive thought. All that fancy produces depends on former impressions of sense. It is powerless to create anything new; its products are mere combinations in memory of the residua of former impressions. They may be unlikely enough, and in that sense it may be true that its products are "original"; but this does not conflict with the facts alleged. It is this creative and somewhat independent power of fancy which lends to the work of art its character of originality, and hence it is that many inquirers have found in that the essence of genius.

The psychological analysis of famous poets will show that the intellectual function is no whit less important a factor of poetic genius than fancy itself, although the latter is the one immediately employed in the act of composition. We have seen that creative fancy works with the material which former impressions of sense have left behind as their remains or residua. The more comprehensive the knowledge of the poet, therefore, and the more he is in condition to assimilate and compact the impressions the world conveys to him, and the sounder and truer his judgments of persons and situations, and the more methodical his thought and the better his memory, by so much the more will his fancy display luxuriance, and so much more various will be his creations. Another psychical phenomenon, besides fancy and intellectual function, surprises us in famous poets—to wit, a refinement of the feelings, heart, and moods. We often find these qualities developed in great poets to a point we can scarcely imagine. Another trait remarkable in famous poets is an instinctive and invincible impulse to express the ideas and feelings within them. In consequence of this impulse, the work of genius is not a voluntary labor, but the "involuntary product of a psychical need. It is not a hankering after applause and success, nor a regard for his other interests, which induces the man of genius to perform his task. It is solely a passion to give shape and form to the idea that exists in his fancy. The true poet does not versify because he would, but because he must. The comparison of traits applied to a considerable number of typical "men of genius" leads to the conclusion that the word does not express any one psychological concept, and that nobody has succeeded in giving a pregnant definition of the quality or is likely to do so. As insanity is equally indefinable, and it is impossible to draw a sharp line between mental sanity and mental derangement, it may seem useless to attempt to compare two such indefinite quantities; still, the comparison may possibly enrich our knowledge and lead us toward a recognition of the truth.

It is no newfangled notion that genius and insanity are connected. It has been reiterated from Plato down. The chief condition of mental sanity is a well-proportioned development of the different psychical factors. But as in the development of the different mental faculties, so also in their proportion to one another, a certain latitude of health is to be allowed. In one man fancy is preponderant; in another, consecutive thought; while a third may have particularly strong feelings as his characteristic. Yet we have no reason to say that these minds transgress the border of health. It is the difference in the relation of the different psychical elements that makes the diversity of men's characters. Now, we know that there are no two characters in the world that are precisely alike. It follows that there is no norm for these relations. The higher the grade of development of the genius and of the individual, the more prominent will differences of psychical factors become, and a correspondingly greater latitude of health must be allowed.

A comparison is instituted between the different symptoms of exaggerated proportions in development which have been discovered in great men, and an endeavor to ascertain the distinctions between these and symptoms of insanity. Among these symptoms are hallucinations, to which the soundest of men have been found more or less subject, over-exuberance of fancy, and self-abandonment in the restless strife for some ideal goal. In great artists and scholars, on the one hand, and in the insane on the other, there is a great, irresistible impulse which fills them to overflowing and makes them forget all personal considerations. But while in the former the restless compulsion to create, the hot aspiration is the kernel of the highest and noblest perfection of man, in the latter there is a morbid impulse which is usually directed to the silliest things. Formerly such a state was called a monomania, since this irresistible impulse seemed to be the only pathological symptom; but careful observation has shown that there is always a more general psychical malady, usually the consequence of arrested development. It is perfectly astonishing with what tenacity and untiring persistence such, patients go to work.

Those patients exhibit the same phenomena who may be termed inventors and Utopians. They not seldom sacrifice their means and bring themselves and their families to ruin by their unconquerable desire of making inventions and discoveries. They are fully convinced, in their folly, of the epoch-making importance of their improvements, and all pains are lost to cause them to desist from their ridiculous performances. In contrast with students, in whom the turning point of their mental action lies in the understanding, in artists moods and feelings are often the starting point of their productions. Hence we find that in them this part of the mental organ has not infrequently an enormous development. As with the other psychical characters, so likewise here we find that the high refinement of a single factor—always, however, in just proportion to the total action of the organ—produces outward phenomena having some similarity with those states which are due to disturbed inward equilibrium, and which we often have occasion to observe in the insane.

No doubt, poets and artists, as well as scholars, often exhibit an outward appearance of self-absorption and of indifference to their surroundings. This is common to them with many of the insane. But how disparate are the causes underlying these phenomena! With the weak-minded it is the want of power to concentrate the attention which renders them uninterested and indifferent to the outward world; but with poets and scholars it is, on the contrary, the high degree of that power which brings about similar phenomena. As we know, the centrifugal condition which we term attention not only extends its power to the organ of sense whose action is emphasized, but it must also be able to order off all the rest of the impressions of sense. The great thinker appears uninterested in surrounding things because his whole attention is directed to the well-ordered sequence of his logical thoughts, to which end, with fullest consciousness, the outward impressions are ordered off. The weak-minded man is present at a performance. The sounds of the words of the orator ring in his ears, but the slightest outward or inward impression suffices to make his attention wander. His thoughts ramble. They are everywhere and nowhere. The mentally gifted man, on the contrary, constantly has his mind on the matter in hand. If he wishes to concentrate his thoughts upon an outward object, nothing that takes place is able to escape him. Neither the psychologist nor the psychiatrist ought to be content to observe behavior superficially, but must trace out the motive of it in order to draw any inference from it. The most absurd conduct sometimes has reasons consistent with health, while conduct which would not surprise a layman at all may be regarded by a psychiatrist as a well-recognized symptom of insanity.

A further explanation of many peculiarities of men of genius is to be sought in their relations to the society in which they live. A man with a reputation for high talents, distinguished from his youth for his superiority and genius, always has his circle of admirers with its proportion of flatterers. If he had the misfortune to be a precocious child, he will have been accustomed from his earliest youth to the idea that his genius is far above ordinary men and above the rules that apply to those men. If such a man is, in later years, attacked by a competent critic upon this or that point, or if schools and parties are formed unfavorable to his method, whether in art or in science, he will, of course, react otherwise than a man would do who was accustomed to opposition of every description. He will, perhaps, regard his just critic as a personal enemy; he will complain that he is misunderstood by his contemporaries, and his passion may go so far that the public at large and superficial observers among psychiatrists may consider him to be the victim of a delusion of persecution.

Peculiar inclinations and other mental idiosyncrasies of men of genius can mostly be very readily explained. Everybody accustomed psychologically to study and dissect those whom he meets, so far as opportunity is afforded, is familiar with the remark that each individual of the human race has his peculiarities, more or less odd, his "weaknesses." The ordinary man, if he has the least breeding, has been accustomed from his youth up to hold in check one inclination or another which violates the usages of society, or even perhaps of good morals. He has learned to attend sufficiently to his own conduct not to allow habits to take root which might appear unusual or be disagreeable to others. But the man of genius is far too much governed by his inward processes, his fancy, and his work to pay attention to trifling details of manner. He therefore appears what he really is, while the average man would not do this. Consequently, chance peculiarities and special inclinations appear in the former more than in the latter.

Thus it is that the behavior of great men is not to be measured by the same standard as that of others, that we have to take account of the motives of their actions, and that the psychical conditions must be kept in view if we are to draw any trustworthy inferences from their behavior. Those mighty natures must be judged from their own organization, and not from, the Philistine point of view of the so-called average man.

As a further proof of the affinity of genius to insanity, it has been alleged that a great number of eminent men have actually had attacks of insanity. But the question is not whether there have been great men who were insane, but whether the proportion of those who have at some period of their lives been attacked by insanity of different types has been markedly greater or less among famous personages than among the general run of mankind. In order to decide this, we should be in a condition to state with exactitude what the percentage of insane among the total population was at a given period of history, how many men of genius there were at that time, and how many of these were insane. Such researches must be repeated at different times of history; then, if they were irreproachably exact and sufficient, it would be possible that some sound conclusion might be reached.

There has also been an attempt to trace a connection between genius and insanity through facts of heredity. In spite of some valuable works in this department, it must be admitted that the observations hitherto adduced are still far from sufficient to have any scientific value. The fact that in several families of eminent men insanity has occurred in no wise justifies us in drawing any conclusion. In order to do that, we must, as in the former case, be in a condition to establish statistical comparisons which shall be *absolutely exact* between the proportionate occurrence of insanity in the families of men of genius and those of ordinary men. Every disinterested observer must be struck with contradictions and the inadequacy of the investigations that have been made in this field.

It is true that between famous men—the so-called geniuses—and the insane many resemblances may be traced. Nevertheless, they are, as we have seen, mere resemblances, not real affinities. Just as every symptom of mental disease has its analogue in health, so has it also an analogue in genius. But, owing to the entire mental action being higher than in average men, the states analogous to morbid symptoms here come out more markedly. Genius resembles insanity as gold resembles brass. The similarity is merely in the appearance. When we go deeper into the facts we find the two states so widely disparate that we are not justified in saying that they are allied; still less, with Moreau, that genius is a morbid condition.

Finally, let the fact be considered that most of the great men, both of art and of science, were misunderstood by their contemporaries, and were only appreciated after they were dead. In recognition of this truth, Goethe pronounces that a genius is in touch with his century only by virtue of his defects, only in so far as he shares the weaknesses of his times. The genius of the truly great man outstrips, with its great wing strokes, the rest of the flock. Those who can not keep up with him can not comprehend him. They are puzzled at first, and finally set him down as a fool. In short, they confound genius and insanity.

Genius and Insanity[2]

The problems which have so long perplexed the thoughtful mind in presence of that dark yet fascinating mystery, the nature and origin of genius, have recently propounded themselves with new stress and insistence. Whatever may be said against Mr. Froude's neglect of the pruning-knife in publishing Carlyle's "Journals and Letters," the psychologist at least will be grateful to him for what is certainly an unusually full and direct presentment of the temperament and life of genius. Here we may study the strange lineaments which

2 By Sully James.

stamp a family likeness on the selected few in whose souls has burned the genuine fire of inspiration. These memoirs disclose with a startling distinctness the pathetic as well as the heroic side of the great man. In Carlyle we see the human spirit in its supreme strength jarred and put out of tune by the suffering incident to preternaturally keen sensibilities and an unalterably gloomy temperament.

In this strange record, too, we find ourselves once more face to face with what is perhaps the most fascinating of the fascinating problems surrounding the subject of intellectual greatness, that of its relation to mental health. Carlyle compels the attentive reader to propound to himself anew the long-standing puzzle, "Is genius somethingwholly normal and sane?" For there is surely a suggestion of temporary mental unsoundness in the idea of that lonely wanderer through the crowded streets of London suddenly seeing in the figures he met so many specters, and feeling himself to be but another "ghastly phantom haunted by demons." And, if all anger is a sort of madness, it is but natural that one should see something of a momentary mania in those terrible outbursts of a spirit of revolt against all things which now and again made desolate the Chelsea home, and wrung from the sage's wife the humiliating confession that she felt as if she were "keeper in a madhouse."

The idea that there is an affinity between genius and mental disease seems at first foreign to our modern habits of thought. In the one, we have human intellect rejoicing in Titanic strength; in the other, that same intellect disordered and pitiably enfeebled. Yet, as has been hinted, the belief in the connection of the two is an old and persistent one. In truth, the common opinion has always gravitated toward this belief. A word or two may make this clear.

To the multitude of men genius wears a double aspect. Superlative intellectual endowment is plainly something very unlike the ordinary type of intelligence. The relation of lofty superiority includes that of distance, and mediocrity in viewing the advent of some new spiritual star may adopt either the one or the other *manière de voir.* Which aspect it will select for special contemplation depends on circumstances. In general it may be said that, since the recognition of greatness presupposes a power of comprehension not always granted to mediocrity, the fact of distance is more likely to impress than the fact of altitude. It is only when supreme wisdom has justified itself, as in the predictions of the true prophet, that its essential Tightness is seen by the crowd.

Otherwise the great man has had to look for recognition mainly from his peers and the slightly more numerous company of those whose heads rise above the mists of contemporary prejudice.

It is easy to see that this vulgar way of envisaging genius as marked divergence from common-sense views of things may lead on to a condemnation of it as a thing unnatural and misshapen. For, evidently, such divergence bears a superficial likeness to eccentricity. Indeed, ' as has been well said, the original teacher has this much in common with the man mentally deranged, that he "is in a minority of one"; and, when pains are not taken to note the direction of the divergence, originality may readily be confounded with the most stupid singularity; and, further, a cursory glance at the constitution of genius will suffice to show that the originator of new and startling ideas is very apt to shock the sense of common men by eccentricities in his manner of life. A man whose soul is being consumed by the desire to discover some new truth, or to give shape to some new artistic idea, is exceedingly liable to fall below the exactions of conventional society in the matter of toilet and other small businesses of life. Among the many humorously pathetic incidents in the records of great men, there is perhaps none more touching than the futile attempt of Beethoven to dress himself with scrupulous conformity to the Viennese pattern of his day.

In contradistinction to this disparaging view, the admiring contemplation of the great man as towering above minds of ordinary stature seems directly opposed to any approximation of the ideas of genius and mental disorder. And this has undoubtedly been in the main the tendency of the more intelligent kind of reverence. At the same time, by a strange, eddy-like movement in the current of human thought, the very feeling for the marvelousness of genius has given birth to a theory of its nature which in another way has associated it with mental aberration. I refer to the ancient doctrine of inspiration as developed more particularly in Greece.

It may be worth while to review for a moment the general course of thought on this dark subject.

In the classic world, preternatural intellectual endowments were, on the whole, greeted with admiration. In Greece more particularly, the fine esthetic sense for what is noble, and the quenchless thirst for new ideas, led to a revering appreciation of great original powers. The whole manner of viewing such gifts was charged with supernaturalism. As the very words employed clearly indicate, such fine native endowment was attributed to the superior quality of the protective spirit (*δαίμων*, genius) which attended each individual from his birth. We see this supernaturalism still more plainly in the Greek notion of the process of intellectual generation. The profound mystery of the process, hardly less deep than that of physical generation, led to the grand supposition of a direct action of the Deity on the productive mind. To the Greeks the conception of new artistic ideas implied a possession (*κατοχή*) of the individual spirit by the god.

Now, it might naturally occur to one that such an inundation of the narrow confines of the human mind by the divine fullness would produce a violent disturbance of its customary processes. It was a shock which agitated the whole being to its foundation, exciting it to a pitch of frenzy or mania. The poet was conceived of as infuriated or driven mad by the god; and a somewhat analogous effect of divine intoxication was recognized by Plato as constituting the essence of philosophic intuition. Hence Greek and Roman literature abounds with statements and expressions which tend to assimilate the man of genius to a madman. The "furor poeticus" of Cicero and the "amabilis insania" of Horace answer to the θεια μανια of Plato. And to the more scientific mind of Aristotle it appeared certain (according to Seneca) that there was no great intellect (*magnum ingenium*) without some mixture of madness (*dementiæ*).

It must be remembered, however, that in the eyes of the ancients genius was hardly degraded by this companionship with madness. Men had not yet begun to look on insanity as one of the most pitiable of maladies. So far from this, it was a common idea that the insane were themselves inspired by the action of deity. We have a striking illustration of the absence even among the educated Greeks of the modern feeling toward madness in the fact that Plato was able to argue, with no discoverable trace of his playful irony, that certain sorts of madness are to be esteemed a good rather than an evil.

The influence of Christianity and of the Church served at first to brand mental derangement with the mark of degradation. The doctrine of possession now assumed a distinctly repellent form by the introduction of the Oriental idea of an evil spirit taking captive the human frame and using it as an instrument of its foul purposes. The full development of this idea of demoniacal possession in the middle ages led, as we know, to many cruelties. And, though Christianity showed its humane side in making provision for the insane by asylums, the treatment of mental disease during this period was, on the whole, marked by much harshness.

This debasement of the idea of madness had, however, no appreciable effect in dissolving the companionship of the two ideas in popular thought. For the attitude of the Church was, for the most part, hostile to new ideas, and so to men of original power. In sooth, we know that they were again and again branded as heretics, and as wicked men possessed by the devil. And thus genius was attached to insanity by a new bond of kinship.

The transition to the modern period introduces us to a new conception both of genius and of insanity. The impulse of inquisitiveness, the delight in new ideas, aided by the historical spirit with its deep sense of indebtedness to the past, have led the later world to extol intellectual greatness. We have learned to see in it the highest product of Nature's organic energy, the last and greatest miracle of evolution. On the other hand, the modern mind has ceased to see in insanity a supernatural agency, and in assimilating it to other forms of disease has taken up a humane and helpful attitude toward it.

Such a change of view might seem at first to necessitate a sharp severance of the new ideas. For, while it places genius at the apex of evolution, it reduces madness to a form of disintegration and dissolution. Nevertheless, we meet in modern literature with an unmistakable tendency to maintain the old association of ideas. Genius is now recognized as having a pathological side, or a side related to mental disease. Among our own writers we have so healthy and serene a spirit as Shakespeare asserting a degree of affinity between poetic creation and madness:

> "The lunatic, the lover, and the poet,
> Are of imagination all compact, etc…"
>
> Midsummer-Night's Dream, act v, sc. 1.

A more serious affirmation of a propinquity is to be found in the well known lines of Dryden:

> "Great wits are sure to madness near
> allied,
> And thin partitions do their bounds
> divide."

As might be expected, French writers, with their relish for pungent paradox, have dealt with special fullness on this theme. "Infinis esprits," writes Montaigne on a visit to Tasso in his asylum, "se trouvent ruinez par leur propre force et soupplesse." Pascal observes that "l'extrême esprit est voisin de l'extrême folie." In a similar strain Diderot writes: "Oh! que le génie et la folie se touchent de bien près!" The French writer who most distinctly emphasizes the proposition is Lamartine. "Le génie," he observes in one place, "porte en lui un principe de destruction, de mort, de *folie,* comme le fruit porte le ver"; and again he speaks of that

47

"maladie mentale" which is called genius.

In German literature it is Goethe, the perfect ideal, as it would seem, of healthy genius, who dwells most impressively on this idea. His drama, "Tasso," is an elaborate attempt to uncover and expose the morbid growths which are apt to cling parasitically about the tender plant of genius. With this must be mentioned, as another striking literary presentment of the same subject, the two eloquent passages on the nature of genius in Schopenhauer's *opus magnum.*

Against this compact consensus of opinion on the one side we have only a rare protest like that of Charles Lamb on behalf of the radical sanity of genius, Such a mass of opinion can not lightly be dismissed as valueless. It is impossible to set down utterances of men like Diderot or Goethe to the envy of mediocrity. Nor can we readily suppose that so many penetrating intellects have been misled by a passion for startling paradox. We are to remember, moreover, that this is not a view of the great man *ab extra,* like that of the vulgar already referred to; it is the opinion of members of the distinguished fraternity themselves who are able to observe and study genius from the inside.

Still, it may be said, this is, after all, only unscientific opinion. Has Science, with her more careful method of investigating and proving, anything to say on this interesting theme? It is hardly to he supposed that she would have overlooked so fascinating a subject. And, as a matter of fact, it has received a considerable amount of attention from pathologists and psychologists. And here for once Science appears to support the popular opinion. The writers who have made the subject their special study agree as to the central fact that there is a relation between high intellectual endowment and mental derangement, though they differ in their way of defining this relation. This conclusion is reached both inductively by a survey of facts, and deductively by reasoning from the known nature and conditions of great intellectual achievement on the one hand, and of mental disease on the other.

What we require first of all is clearly as many instances as can be found of men of genius who have exhibited intellectual or moral peculiarities which are distinctly symptomatic of mental disease. Such a collection of facts, if sufficient, will supply us with a basis for induction. In making this collection we need not adopt any theory respecting the nature either of genius or of mental disease. It is sufficient to ay that we include under the former term all varieties of originative power, whether in art, science, or practical affairs. And as to the latter term, it is enough to start with the assumption that fully developed insanity is recognizable by certain well-known marks; and that there are degrees of mental deterioration, and a gradual transition from mental health to mental disease, the stages of which also can, roughly at least, be marked off and identified.

In surveying the facts which have been relied on by writers, we shall lay most stress on mental as distinguished from bodily or nervous symptoms. And of these we may conveniently begin with the less serious manifestations:

1. The lowest grade of mental disturbance is seen in that temporary appearance of irrationality which comes from an extreme state of "abstraction" or

absence of mind. To the vulgar, as already hinted, all intense preoccupation with ideas, by calling off the attention from outer things and giving a dream-like appearance to the mental state, is apt to appear symptomatic of "queerness" in the head. But in order that it may find a place among distinctly abnormal features this absence of mind must attain a certain depth and persistence. The ancient story of Archimedes, and the amusing anecdotes of Newton's fits, if authentic, might be said perhaps to illustrate the border-line between a normal and an abnormal condition of mind. A more distinctly pathological case is that of Beethoven, who could not be made to understand why his standing in his night attire at an open window should attract the irreverent notice of the street boys. For in this case we have a temporary incapacity to perceive exterior objects and their relations; and a deeper incapacity of a like nature clearly shows itself in poor Johnson's standing before the town clock vainly trying to make out the hour.

This same aloofness of mind from the external world betrays itself in many of the eccentric habits attributed to men and women of genius. Here, again, Johnson serves as a good instance. His inconvenient habit of suddenly breaking out with scraps of the Lord's Prayer in a fashionable assembly marks a distinctly dangerous drifting away of the inner life from the firm anchorage of external fact.

In the cases just considered we have to do with a kind of mental blindness to outer circumstances. A further advance along the line of intellectual degeneration is seen in the persistence of vivid ideas, commonly anticipations of evil of some kind, which have no basis in external reality. Johnson's dislike to particular alleys in his London walks, and Madame de Staël's *bizarre* idea that she would suffer from cold when buried, may be taken as examples of these painful delusions or *idées fixes*. A more serious stage of such delusions is seen in the case of Pascal, who is said to have been haunted by the fear of a gulf yawning just in front of him, which sometimes became so overmastering that he had to be fastened by a chain to keep him from leaping forward.

It is plain that in this last case we touch on the confines of sense-illusion. It is probable that hallucinations may occur as very rare experiences in the case of normal and healthy minds. Yet, though not confined to states of insanity, illusions of the senses are commonly, if not always, indicative of at least a temporary disturbance of the psycho-physical organism. And we have on record a considerable number of instances of eminent men who were subject to these deceptions. It is not only the religious recluse, with his ill-nourished body, and his persistent withdrawal from the corrective touch of outer things, who experiences them. Luther was their victim as well as Loyola. Auditory hallucinations—that is, the hearing of imaginary voices—appear to have occurred to Malebranche and Descartes, as they certainly did to Johnson. The instances of visual hallucinations are perhaps more numerous still. Pope, Johnson, Byron, Shelley, are said to have had their visions. Even so strong and well-balanced a mind as Goethe was not exempted. Nor has the active life of the soldier always proved a safeguard. The stories of the prognostic visions of Brutus and other generals of the old world are well known. Among modern ones, Napoleon is said to have had recurring visits from his guardian spirit or genius.

In the abnormalities just touched on, disturbance of intellectual function is the chief circumstance, though an element of emotional disturbance is commonly observable as well. In another class of cases this last ingredient becomes the conspicuous feature. By this is meant such an accession of general emotional excitability, and along with this such a hypertrophy and absolute ascendency of certain feelings, as to constitute a distinct approximation to the disorganized psychical state which has been called moral insanity.

And here reference may first be made to that violence of temper and that extravagant projection of self and its concerns to the displacement of others' claims and interests which might be termed a kind of moral hallucination. How many names in the roll of English writers at once occur to the mind in this connection! Pope, Johnson, Swift, Byron, to which list must now be added Carlyle, may be taken as typical instances of the *genus irritabile vatum.* And among foreign deities we have Voltaire and Rousseau, Handel and Beethoven, and even philosophers like Herder and Schopenhauer.

Other emotional disorders take on more distinctly the aspect of moral obliquities. And here we have specially to do with poetic genius. Without adopting the slightly contemptuous opinion that poets are, as a rule, a "sensuous, erotic race," one must admit that an untamed wildness of amatory passion has been a not infrequent accompaniment of fine poetic imagination.

For a clear illustration, however, of the morbid tendency of such irregularities, we must go, not to the comparatively regular life of a Goethe or a Shelley, but to the wild and lawless career of a Rousseau, of whom it was well said by a clever woman, "*Quand la Nature forma Rousseau, la sagesse pétrit la pâte, mais la folie y jeta son levain.*"

To a tempestuous violence of sexual passion there has too commonly joined itself a feverish craving for physical stimulants; and so the pure heavenly flame of genius has again and again had to contend with the foul, murky vapors which exhale from the lower animal nature. No need to tell again the gloomy story of splendid power eaten into and finally destroyed by the cancer of rampant appetite. In our own literature the names of Ben Jonson, Nat Lee, Burns, and others at once occur to the student. Edgar Allan Poe represents the same tragic fatefulness of genius in American letters. Among Frenchmen we have as conspicuous examples Villon and De Musset. Among Germans,

Günther, Bürger, and numbers of those about Herder and Goethe in the turbulent times of the *Sturm und Drang,* and Hoffmann, the novelist, suffered the same moral shipwreck.

2. We may now pass to another class of cases in which the pathological character is still more plainly discernible. Outbursts of fierce passionateness may perhaps be thought by some to be, after all, only marks of a certain kind of robust vitality. But no one will say this of the gloomy depression, the melancholy brooding on personal ills, ending sometimes in distinctly hypochondriac despondency, which have not unfrequently been the accompaniment of great intellectual power. It was remarked

by Aristotle, who was a long way the shrewdest and most scientific observer of antiquity, that all men of genius have been melancholic or atrabilious. He instances Empedocles, Socrates, and Plato, and the larger number of the poets. And the page of modern biographic literature would supply many a striking illustration of the same temperament. The pessimism of Johnson, Swift, Byron, and Carlyle, of Schopenhauer and Lenau, of Leopardi and of Lamartine, may perhaps be taken as a signal manifestation of the gloom which is apt to encompass great and elevated spirits, like the mists which drift toward and encircle the highest mountain-peaks.

In some cases this melancholy assumes a more acute form, giving rise to the thought and even the act of suicide. Among those who have confessed to have experienced the impulse may be mentioned Goethe in the Werther days, Beethoven during the depression brought on by his deafness, Chateaubriand in his youth, and George Sand also in her early days. The last, writing of her experience, says, "Cette sensation" (at the sight of water, a precipice, etc.) "fut quelquefois si vive, si subite, si bizarre, que je pus bien constater que c'était une espèce de folie dont j'étais atteinte." Johnson's weariness of life was, it seems certain, only prevented from developing into the idea of suicide by his strong religious feeling and his extraordinary dread of death, which was itself, perhaps, a morbid symptom.

In some cases this idea prompted to actual attempts to take away life. The story of Cowper's trying to hang himself, and afterward experiencing intense religious remorse, is well known. Another instance is that of Saint-Simon, whose enormous vanity itself looks like a form of monomania, and who, in a fit of despondency, fired a pistol at his head, happily with no graver result than the loss of an eye. Alfieri, who was the victim of the "most horrid melancholy," tried on one occasion, after being bled by a surgeon, to tear off the bandage in order to bleed to death. Among those who succeeded in taking away their life are Chatterton, whose mind had been haunted by the idea from early life, Kleist the poet, and Beneke the philosopher.

3. We may now pass to the most important group of facts—namely, instances of men of genius who have suffered from fully developed mental disease.

In certain cases this disruption of the organs of mind shows itself in old age, and here, it is evident, we have to distinguish what is known as senile dementia from the impairment of faculty incident to old age. A clear instance of cerebral disease is afforded by the botanist Linnæus, whose faculties gave way after a stroke. The mental stupor into which the poet Southey finally sank was a similar phenomenon. Swift's fatal disease, the nature of which has only recently been cleared up by science, was cerebral disorganization brought on by peripheral disease in the organ of hearing. Zimmermann, the author of the work on "Solitude," who had been a hypochondriac from the age of twenty, ended his life in a state of melancholy indistinguishable from insanity. The final collapse, under the pressure of pecuniary anxieties, of Scott's cerebral powers, is too well known to need more than a bare mention.

Besides these instances of senile collapse, there are several cases of insanity showing itself in the vigorous period of life. Sometimes, as in the instance of Richelieu, who had shown himself an erratic being from his childhood, the madness appeared as a sudden and transient fit of delirium. In other cases the disorder took a firmer hold on the patient. Charles Lamb, Handel, and Auguste Comte suffered from insanity for a time, and had to be put under restraint. Tasso, whose whole nature was distinctly tinged with the "insane temperament," had again and again to be confined as a madman. Donizetti was also for a time insane and confined in an asylum. Among those who became hopelessly insane were the poets Lenau and Holderlin and the composer Schumann, the latter of whom had long been the victim of melancholy and hallucinations, and had before his confinement attempted to drown himself in the Rhine.

I have preferred to dwell on the physical aspect of the relation between genius and disease. But no adequate investigation of the subject is possible which does not consider the physical aspect as well. No one now, perhaps, really doubts that to every degree of mental disturbance and mental disorganization there corresponds some degree of deterioration and disorganization of the nerve-centers.

Psychical disturbance and disruption proceed *pari passu* with physical.

This being so, it is pertinent to our study to remark that men of genius have in a surprising number of cases been affected by forms of nervous disease which, though not having such well-marked psychical accompaniments as occur in states of insanity, are known to be allied to these.

4. To begin with, it seems certain that a number of great men have died from disease of the nerve-centers. Among other names may be mentioned Pascal, who had all his life been the victim of nervous disorders, and who succumbed, at the early age of thirty-nine, to

paralysis accompanied by convulsions. Two of the greatest scientific men, Kepler and Cuvier, died, according to Moreau, from disease of the brain. Rousseau was carried off by an attack of apoplexy. Mozart's early death was due to brain-disease, showing itself in other ways by morbid delusions, fainting-fits, and convulsions. Another musician, Mendelssohn, succumbed to an attack of apoplexy. Heine's fatal malady, which kept him for seven years a prisoner in his "mattress-grave," was disease of the lower nerve-centers in the spinal cord.

Other men of genius have suffered from nervous disorders from time to time. Molière was the subject of recurring convulsions, an attack of which would prevent his working for fifteen days. Alfieri, to whose morbid mental symptoms reference has already been made, suffered when young from a disease of the lymphatic system, and was afterward liable to convulsions. Paganini, the musician, suffered from an attack of catalepsy when four years old, and later on was the victim of recurring convulsions; and Schiller, who was very delicate from youth, was also the subject of recurring fainting-fits and convulsions.

The lesser forms of nervous disorder—headache, *malaise,* and recurring periods of nervous prostration—are too common among all brain-workers to call for special notice here. The latest biography of a woman of genius strikingly illustrates this milder form of the penalty which mortals have to pay for daring to aspire to the ranks of the immortals. In George Eliot we have one more name added to the list of great ones to whom, to use the words of a French writer, has been granted "le funeste privilège d'entendre crier à toute heure les ressorts de leur machine."

5. One other significant group of facts remains to be touched on. In a considerable number of cases it has been ascertained that insanity or other form of nervous disorder has shown itself in the same family as genius, whether as its forerunner, companion, or successor. Chateaubriand's father is said to have

died of apoplexy. Schopenhauer's grandmother and uncle were imbecile. Several distinguished men had insane sisters, among others Richelieu, Diderot, Hegel, and Charles Lamb. One of Mendelssohn's sons became insane.

I have endeavored in this brief review of the alleged facts to give an adequate impression of their variety and range. It now remains to inquire into their precise evidential value.

The first question that naturally arises here is whether the facts are well authenticated and accurately presented. A cautious mind will readily reflect that if genius as such is apt to assume an abnormal aspect to average common sense, biographers may easily have invented, or at least exaggerated, some of the alleged morbid characteristics of the great; and as a matter of fact there is good reason to suppose that this falsifying of the record of greatness has taken place. I may refer to the story of the madness and suicide of Lucretius, which is extremely doubtful, and may have grown out of a religious horror at the supposed tendency of his writings. The story of Newton's madness, again, which is given by a French biographer, and which is ably refuted by Sir David Brewster, may owe much of its piquancy to what may be called the unconscious inventiveness of prejudice. Very possibly the stories of the visions of Brutus, Cromwell, and others, have had a like origin.

Again, it will be said that even medical men—wishing like others to magnify their office—may have been too ready in spying out the symptoms of insanity. If they are fallible in dealing with the living subject, all of whose physical and mental characteristics are accessible to observation, how much more likely are they to err in diagnosing the minds of the dead by help of a few fragmentary indications only! I think the force of this objection, too, must be allowed. When, for example, a French alienist thinks it worth while to write a book in order to prove that the belief of Socrates in a controlling divinity (xxx

xxx) was a symptom of mental disease, a layman may be pardoned for demanding a mode of investigation more in accordance with the proud claims of science to our absolute and unstinted confidence. A well-informed and critical reader of M. Moreau's tables of biographical facts will not fail to challenge more than one statement of his respecting the morbid characteristics of great men, ancient and modern.

Allowing, however, for a margin of error, I do not think any candid mind will fail to see that such a body of facts as remains is sufficient to justify us in drawing a conclusion. If men of the highest intellectual caliber were not more liable to mental and nervous disorders than others, no such list out of the short roll of great names could have been obtained. No elaborate calculations are needed, I think, to show that mental malady occurs too often in the history of genius.

One might perhaps try to evade the unpalatable conclusion by saying that there is genius and genius; that it is weakly, one-sided, and *bizarre* originality which exhibits these unhealthinesses, whereas the larger and more vigorous productiveness of an Aristotle, a Shakespeare, or a Goethe, is free from such blemishes. I think, however, that our facts will compel us to reject this saving clause. There is no question among competent critics of the splendid quality of genius of Swift, of Carlyle, or of Beethoven. Nor in cases of so-called healthy genius can it be said that nothing abnormal ever shows itself. The above references to Goethe may serve to indicate the liability to abnormal deviation even in the strongest and seemingly most stable type of genius. As for Shakespeare, the instance commonly referred to by Lamb and others who have come to the defense of genius, it is enough to say that our knowledge of his personality and life is far too meager to justify any conclusion on the point.

And this brings us to another very important consideration. If too much has been made of the alleged positive instances, too much has been made also of the apparent contradictions or exceptions. The record of past greatness is far too scanty for the most plodding student to find all cases of morbid symptoms which have presented themselves. We who live in an age when a fierce light beats on the throne of intellect, when the public which genius serves is greedy of every trivial detail of information respecting its behavior in the curtained recess of private life, can hardly understand how our ancestors could have neglected to chronicle and to preserve the words and deeds of the greatest of men. Yet such is the case, and the further we go back the scantier the biographic page. Inasmuch, too, as many of the symptoms of nervous disease in the intellectual heroes themselves or their families would possess no significance to the ordinary lay mind, we may feel confident that in many cases where we have a fairly full record important data are omitted.

Another thought naturally occurs to one in this connection. Without indorsing the ancient proverb that the best men die in their youth, we may find good grounds for conjecturing that many endowed with the gift of genius have passed away before their powers culminated in the production of a great monumental work. The early collapse of so many who did attain fame suggests this conclusion. And among such short-lived and unknown recipients of the divine afflatus it seems reasonable to infer that there were a considerable number who succumbed to some of those forms of psycho-physical disease which have so often attacked their survivors.

It seems, then, to be an irresistible conclusion that the foremost among human intellects have had more than their share of the ills that flesh is heir to. The possession of genius appears in some way to be unfavorable to the maintenance of a robust mental health. And here arises the question how we are to view this connection. Is the

presence of the creative faculty to be regarded as itself an abnormal excrescence in the human mind? Or is it that the possession and fruition of the faculty are apt to be attended with circumstances which are injurious to perfect mental well-being?

In order to understand the precise relation between two things, we ought to know all about the nature and causes of each. But this we are very far from knowing in the present case. Science has, no doubt, done much to clear up the ancient mystery of madness. We now know that it has a perfectly natural origin, and we understand a good deal respecting the more conspicuous agencies, psychical and physical, predisposing and exciting, which bring about the malady. Yet so intricate is the subject, so complex and subtile the influences which may conspire to just disturb the mental balance, that in many cases, even with a full knowledge of an individual and his antecedents, the most skillful expert finds himself unable to give a complete and exhaustive explanation of the phenomenon.

With respect to genius the case is much worse. We may have a clearer intuition of its organic composition than the ancients; we may be able better than they to describe in psychological terms the essential qualities of the original and creative mind. But we have hardly advanced a sate) with respect to a knowledge of its genesis and antecedents. We do, no doubt, know some little about its family history. Mr. Galton, with his characteristic skill in striking out new paths of experimental research, has brought to light a number of interesting facts with respect to the hereditary transmission of high intellectual endowments. But these researches supply no answer to the supremely interesting question, How does the light of genius happen to flash out in this particular family at this precise moment? A preparation there may be, as Goethe somewhere hints, in the patient building up by the family of sterling intellectual and moral virtues. But this is hardly the beginning of an explanation. How much the better are we able to comprehend Carlyle's wondrous gift of spiritual clairvoyance for knowing that he came of a thoroughly sound stock, having more than the average, it may be, of Northern shrewdness? To trace the family characteristics in a great man is one thing, to explain the genius which ennobles and immortalizes these is another.

In the present state of our knowledge, then, genius must be looked upon as the most signal and impressive manifestation of that tendency of Nature to variation and individuation in her organic formations which modern science is compelled to retain among its unexplained facts. Why we have a Shakespeare, a Michael Angelo, a Goethe here and now, is a question that can not be answered. Our ignorance of the many hidden threads that make up the inextricable skein of causation forces us to regard each new appearance of the lamp of genius with much of the wonder, if with something less of the superstition, with which the ancients viewed it.

This being so, we must be content with a very tentative and provisional theory of the relations between genius and mental disease. We can not, for example, follow M. Moreau in his hardy paradox that genius has as its material substratum a semi-morbid state of the brain, a neuropathic constitution which is substantially identical with the "insane temperament" or "insane neurosis." For, first of all, the facts do not support such a generalization. If the "genial temperament" involved a distinct constitutional disposition to insanity, the number of great men who had actually become insane would certainly be much greater than it is. And, in the second place, this proposition reposes on far too unsubstantial a basis of hypothetical neurology. We know too little of the variations of nerve structure and function to pronounce confidently on the essential identity of the nervous organization in the case of the man of genius and of the insane."

A more modest and possibly more hopeful way of approaching the question appears to offer itself in the consideration of the psychical characteristics of genius. We may inquire into those peculiarities of sensibility and emotion, as well as of intellect, which are discoverable in the typical psychical organization of the great man, and may trace out some of the more important reflex influences of the life of intellectual production on his mind and character. What we all recognize as genius displays itself in some large original conception, whether artistic, scientific, or practical. And it seems not improbable that by a closer investigation of the conditions and the results of this large constructive activity of mind we may find a clew to the apparent anomaly that grand intellectual powers are so frequently beset with mental and moral infirmity. These lurking-places of abnormal tendencies will, we may expect, betray themselves more readily in the case of artistic and especially poetic genius, which has, indeed, always been viewed as the most pronounced form, and as the typical representative of creative power.

No careful student of genius can fail to see that it has its roots in a nervous organization of exceptional delicacy. Keenness of sensibility, both to physical and mental stimuli, is one of the fundamental attributes of the original mind. This preternatural sensitiveness of nerve has been illustrated in the two latest records of poetic genius. Carlyle's lively impressibility to sounds and other sensuous agents is familiar to all. And of George Eliot it has been well said that "her nerves were servile to every skyey influence." And what a range and intensity of emotion are at once suggested by names like Milton, Dante, Shelley, Heine!

This fineness of the sentient fiber stands in the closest relation to the intellectual side of genius. It is not so much an accompaniment of the creative imagination as its vitalizing principle. The wide and penetrating vision of the poet is the correlative of his quick, delicate, and many-sided sensibility. And the stimulus which ever urges him toward the ideal region, which makes him devote his days to the pursuit of some ravishing idea, has its origin in his rare, almost superhuman, capacity of feeling. The modest limits of the real world fail to slake his thirst for the delight of beauty, for the raptures of the sublime. Hence the impulse to fashion new worlds of his own. And by such ideal activities the emotional sensibilities which prompted them are deepened and intensified.

It is easy to see, from this glance at the fundamental conditions of imaginative creation, that it has one of its main impulses in uncommon experiences of suffering. The fine nervous organization, tremulously responsive to every touch, constitutes in itself, in this all too imperfect world of ours, a special dispensation of sorrow. Exquisite sensibility seems to be connected with a delicate poise of nervous structure eminently favorable to the experience of jarring and dislocated shock. And it is this preponderance of rude shock over smooth, agreeable stimulation—of a sense of dissonance in things over the joyous consciousness of harmony—which seems to supply one of the most powerful incitants to the life of imagination. Hence the dark streak of melancholy which one so often detects in the early years of the great man.

Such an attitude of mind must entail suffering in other ways, As the biography of the man of genius often tells us, he is apt to become aware, at a painfully early date, that his exceptional endowments and the ardent consuming impulses which belong to them collide with the utilities and purposes of ordinary life. The soul intent on dreaming its secret dream of beauty is unfit for the business which makes up the common working life of plain, prosaic men. The youth to whom the 'embodiment of a noble artistic idea or the discovery of a large, fructifying, moral truth is the one absorbing interest, will be apt to take a shockingly low view of banking, schoolmastering, and the other respectable occupations of ordinary citizens.

It follows that the man of genius is, by his very constitution and vocation, to a considerable extent a solitary. He is apt to offend the world into which he was born by refusing to bow the knee to its conventional deities. His mood of discontent with things presents itself as a reflection on their contented view. On the other hand, his peculiar leanings and aspirations are incomprehensible to them, and stamp him as an alien. "Il y a peu de vices," says Chamfort, with a grim irony, "qui empechent un homme d'avoir beaucoup d'amis, autant que peuvent le faire de trop grandes qualités." Hence the profound solitude of so many of the earth's great ones, which even the companionships of the home have not sufficed to fill up. And it must be remembered that the ardent emotions of the man of genius bring their extra need of sympathy. Even the consciousness of intellectual dissent from others may become to a deeply sympathetic nature an anguish. "I believe you know" (writes Leopardi to a friend), "but I hope you have not experienced, how thought can crucify and martyrize any one who thinks somewhat differently from others."

Such isolation is distinctly unfavorable to mental health. It deprives a man of wholesome contact with others' experience and ideas, and disposes to abnormal eccentricities of thought. It profoundly affects the emotional nature, breeding melancholy, suspicion of others, misanthropy, and other unwholesome progeny. The "strange interior *tomb* life" of which Carlyle speaks is a striking example of the influence of this isolation in fostering the minute germs of morbid delusion.

If now we turn to the process of intellectual origination, we shall find new elements of danger, new forces adverse to the perfect serenity of mental health. If the rich biographical literature of modern times teaches us anything, it is that original production is the severest strain of human faculty, the most violent and exhausting form of cerebral action. The pleasing fiction that the perfectly-shaped artistic product occurs to the creative mind as a kind of happy thought is at once dispelled by a little study of great men's recorded experience. All fine original work, it may be safely said, represents severe intellectual labor on the part of the producer, not necessarily at the moment of achievement, but at least in a preparatory collection and partial elaboration of material. The rapidity with which Scott threw off his masterpieces of fiction is only understood by remembering how he had steeped his imagination for years in the life, the scenery, and the history of his country.

It is to be remembered, too, that this swift and seemingly facile mode of creation is by no means an easy play of faculty, akin to the spontaneous sportiveness of witty talk. It involves the full tension of the mental powers, the driving of the cerebral machine at full speed. According to the testimony of more than one man of genius, this fierce activity is fed and sustained by violent emotional excitement. The notion of producing a work of high imaginative power in a state of perfect cold blood is, as Plato long ago pointed out, absurd. Spiritual generation only takes place when the soul burns and throbs as with a fever. At the moment of productive inspiration the whole being is agitated to its depths, and the latent deposits of years of experience come to the surface. This full spring-tide of imagination, this cerebral turmoil and clash of currents, makes the severest demands on the controlling and guiding forces of volition. And it is only when the mind is capable of the highest effort of sustained concentration that the process of selecting and organizing can keep pace with the rapid inflow of material. Hence, though the excitement may in certain cases be intensely pleasurable, it is nearly always fatiguing and wearing.

But great artistic works are not always flashed into the world by this swift electric process. Some books that men will not let die have been the result of lengthened toil troubled by many a miserable check and delay. The record of Carlyle's experience sufficiently illustrates the truth that there is no necessary relation between rapidity of invention and execution and artistic value of result, Much depends on the passing mood, more still on the temperament of the individual artist. There are others besides Carlyle to whom spiritual parturition has been largely an experience of suffering, the pangs being but rarely submerged in the large, joyous consciousness that a new idea is born into the world. And when this is so there is another kind of strain on the mental machine. The struggle with intellectual obstacle, the fierce passionate resolve to come *in's Heine* which every student experiences in a humble way, becomes something for the spectator to tremble at.

Is it surprising that such states of mental stress and storm should afterward leave the subject exhausted and prostrate? The wild excitement of production is apt to dull the sense still further to the prosaic enjoyments with which ordinary mortals have to content themselves. More than this, the long and intense preoccupation with the things of the imagination is apt to induce a certain lethargy and stupor of the senses, in which the sharp outlines of reality are effaced in a misty, dream-like phantasmagoria. The reader of Carlyle's "Memoirs" need not be reminded how plainly all this appears in his experience. Even the warm and gladdening ray of dawning prosperity failed to cheer him in these hours of spiritual collapse. And he exclaims in one place that there is no other pleasure and possession for him but that of feeling himself working and alive.

In addition to these adverse forces, which have their origin in the common conditions of the life of genius, there are others which, though less constant, present themselves very frequently in co-operation with the first. It has often been remarked that the man of decided originality of thought, being as it were one born out of due time, has to bear the strain of production for a while uncheered by the smile of recognition. And when there is great originality, not only in the ideas, but in the form of expression, such recognition may come too slowly to be of any remunerative value. Neglect or ridicule is the form of greeting which the world has often given to the propounder of a new truth; and where, as frequently happens, the want of instant recognition means the pressure of poverty, which chafes with unusual severity the delicate fibers of sensitive men, we have a new and considerable force added to the agencies which threaten to undermine the not too stable edifice of the great man's mental and moral constitution. Johnson, Lessing, Burns, Leopardi, and many another name, will here occur to those familiar with the lives of modern men of letters.

In view of this combination of threatening agencies, one begins to understand the many eloquent things which have been said about the fatality of great gifts. Thus one finds a meaning in the definition of poetic genius given by Lamartine when speaking of Byron—"a vibration of the human fiber as strong as the heart of man can bear without breaking."

It is not meant here that even when all these destructive elements are present a distinctly pathological condition of mind must necessarily ensue. Their effect may be fully counteracted by other and resisting agencies. Of these the two most important are bodily energy and health on the one hand, and strength of will or character on the other. Where these are both found in a high degree of perfection, as in Goethe, we have a splendid example of healthy genius. On the other hand, if either, and still more if both of these are wanting, we have a state of things which is exceedingly likely to develop a distinctly pathological state of mind.

How, it may be asked, does it commonly fare with the world's intellectual heroes with respect to these means of defense? As to the physical defense, it is known that a number of great men have had a physique fairly adequate to the severe demands made on the nervous organization. They were men of powerful frame, strong muscles, and good digestion. But such robustness of bodily health seems by no means the common rule. The number of puny and ill-formed men who have achieved marvelous things in intellectual production is a fact which has often been remarked on. So common an accompaniment of great intellectual exertion is defective digestion, that aningenious writer has tried to show that the maladies of genius have their main source in dyspepsia. No Englishman, in thinking of this question, can fail to recollect that the three of his countrywomen who have given most distinct proof of creative power— Charlotte Brontë, Mrs. Browning, and George Eliot—were hampered with a physical frame pitiably unequal to support the cerebral superstructure.

Coming now to the moral defense, the thought at once suggests itself that, according to the testimony of more than one writer, genius consists in preternatural force of will more than in anything else. It is, we are told, only the man with an infinite capacity to take pains who is truly great. The prolonged, intense concentration of mind which precedes the final achievement is a severe exertion and striking manifestation of will.

At the same time, a moment's thought will show us that this patient mental incubation is no proof of the higher qualities of will and moral character. The appropriateness of the old way of speaking of creative inspiration as a possession is seen in the fact that the will has little to do with bringing on the condition. "The author," said Lord Beaconsfield, on one occasion, "is a being with a predisposition which with him is irresistible, a bent which he can not in any way avoid, whether it drags him to the abstruse researches of erudition, or induces him to mount into the feverish and turbulent atmosphere of imagination." This sense of a *quasi-*exterior pressure and compulsion is attested by more than one child of genius. In some cases, more particularly, perhaps, among "tone-poets," we find this mastery of the individual mind by the creative impulse assuming the striking form of a sudden abstraction of the thoughts from the surroundings of the moment. And, throughout the whole of the creative process, the will, though, as we have seen, exercised in a peculiarly severe effort, is not exercised fully and in its highest form. There is no deliberate choice of activity here. The man does not feel free to stop or to go on. On the contrary, the will is in this case pressed into the service of the particular emotion that strives for utterance, the particular artistic impulse that is irresistibly bent on self-realization. There is nothing here of the higher moral effort of will, in choosing what we are not at the moment inclined to, and resisting the seductive force of extraneous excitants.

These fragmentary remarks may help us to understand the facts of the case. A certain proportion of great thinkers and artists have shown moral as well as intellectual heroism. Men who were able to take the destruction of a MS. representing long and wearisome research, as Newton and Carlyle took it, must have had something of the stuff of which the stoutest character is woven. The patient upbearing against hardship of men like Johnson and Lessing is what gives the moral relish to the biography of men of letters. More than one intellectual leader, too, has shown the rare quality of practical wisdom. Goethe's calm strength of will, displaying itself in a careful ordering of the daily life, is matter of common knowledge. Beethoven managed just to keep himself right by resolute bodily exercise. In George Eliot an exceptional feeling of moral responsibility sufficed for a nice economizing of the fitful supply of physical energy.

At the same time, our slight study of the ways of genius has familiarized us with illustrations of striking moral weaknesses. We have seen a meaning in Rochefoucauld's paradox, that "il n'appartient qu'aux grands hommes d'avoir de grands défauts." The large draught of mental energy into the channels of imaginative production is apt to leave the will ill-provided in working out the multifarious tasks of a temperate and virtuous life.

Our conclusion is, that the possession of genius carries with it special liabilities to the action of the disintegrating forces which environ us all. It involves a state of delicate equipoise, of unstable equilibrium, in the psycho-physical organization. Paradoxical as it may seem, one may venture to affirm that great original power of mind is incompatible with nice adjustment to surroundings, and so with perfect well-being. And here it is that we see the real qualitative difference between genius and talent. This last means superior endowment in respect of the common practical intelligence which all men understand and appraise. The man of talent follows the current modes of thought, keeps his eye steadily fixed on the popular eye, produces the kind of thing which hits the taste of the moment, and is never guilty of the folly of abandoning himself to the intoxicating excitement of production. To the original inventor of ideas and molder of new forms of art this intoxication is, as we have seen, everything. He is under a kind of divine behest to make and fashion something new and great, and at the moment of compliance recks little of the practical outcome to himself. And such recklessness is clearly only one form of imprudence, and so of mal-adaptation.

But, if improvident, he is improvident in a high cause. Emerson and others have taught us the uses of the great man. The teacher of a new truth, the discoverer of a higher and worthier form of artistic expression, is one in advance of his age, who, by his giant exertions, enables the community, and even the whole race, to reach forward to a further point in the line of intellectual evolution. He is a scout who rides out well in advance of the intellectual army, and who by this very advance and isolation from the main body is exposed to special perils. Thus genius, like philanthropy or conscious self-sacrifice for others, is a mode of variation of human nature which, though unfavorable to the conservation of the individual, aids in the evolution of the species.

If this be a sound view of the nature and social function of the man of genius, it may teach more than one practical lesson. Does it not, for example, suggest that there is room just now for more consideration in dealing with the infirmities of great men? There is no need of exonerating intellectual giants from the graver human responsibilities. We do well to remember that genius has its own special responsibilities, that *noblesse oblige* here too. At the same time we shall do well also to keep in mind that the life of intellectual creation has its own peculiar besetments, and that in the very task of fulfilling his high and eminently humane mission, and giving the world of his mind's best, the great man may become unequal to the smaller fortitudes of every-day life. To judge of the degree of blameworthiness of faults of temper is a nice operation, which may even transcend the ability of a clever and practiced critic. Perhaps the temper most appropriate to the contemplation of genius, and most conducive to fairness of moral judgment, is one in which reverence is softened by personal gratitude, and this last made more completely human by a touch of regretful pity.